# Learned
# It
# In
# Queens

*Digital overload side effects.*

*Photo Credit - Alex Berg*

# The Learned-it-in-Queens Communications Playbook

*Winning Against Digital Distraction*

by Julienne B. Ryan

The Learned-it-in-Queens Communication Playbook



Quantity sales and special discounts are available on quantity purchases by corporations, associations, and others. For details, contact the publisher at the address above.

Orders by U.S. trade bookstores and wholesalers. Email info@ BeyondPublishing.net

The Beyond Publishing Speakers Bureau can bring authors to your live event. For more information or to book an event contact the Beyond Publishing Speakers Bureau speak@BeyondPublishing.net

Cover design and visual by Chad Spader, photo by Alex Berg.

The Author can be reached directly at Jryanpartners.com and BeyondPublishing.net

Manufactured and printed in the United States of America distributed globally by BeyondPublishing.net

New York | Los Angeles | London | Sydney

ISBN Softcover:
ISBN Hardcover:

# Acknowledgments

Most of all, I want to thank and acknowledge my husband, Joe Ryan for his support of me and my work, but I also gratefully acknowledge the many other people who supported my personal growth and helped me find my voice: Dr. Stephen Blau, Dr. Sylvia J. Barsion, Dr. Connie Maria DePinho, Dr. Roseanne L. Flores, Kim Freithaler, Julie Jansen, Debbie O'Connor, Dr. Harriet S. Mosatche, Jeff Rock, and Michele Wood. A special thanks to Sarah Asebrook, who served as my proofreader, Chad Spader, who prepared all my photos, and to Tom Sparough, who served as my senior editor, Kirk Kirkpatrick, who served as my editor and sounding board for the workbook section, Trisha Griffin-Carty who served as a workbook participant and editor, Jan Zucker who reformatted my updated version, and to my Launch 1000 group for listening to my "ideas" and my wonderful network of people who take the time to listen, cheer me on and champion my work in wonderful and amazing ways. Finally, I want to acknowledge my brother Walt Pechulis, Jr., who helped with the photography of the food and who is always sharing his "lessons learned" about growing up in Queens.

# Contents

# Preface

I couldn't wait to leave the borough of Queens, New York when I was growing up. It was full of people and neighborhoods where *nothing* exciting ever happened.

For me, Manhattan was *the* place to be and where *real* New Yorkers lived doing interesting and important things.

I promised myself that as soon as I could, I would escape, and go live in the *The City*—as us residents of Queens called it. So I started to prepare for my departure at an early age, treating forays into *The City* like training expeditions that would allow me to blend in with its natives when I got older.

Eventually, I got my wish and spent time living in New York City in a variety of dwellings, as an au pair in a luxury apartment building on the Upper West Side, and as a sub-letting tenant in a Hell's Kitchen walk-up apartment *before* it got gentrified. Later, I moved to the Bronx and lived in the Bainbridge and Woodlawn neighborhoods. I then exiled myself and crossed over the New York City border into Westchester County. There I assumed the identity of a suburban home owner and commuter.

But as the years passed, I started to think about my childhood in Queens and how living in that borough had impacted my way of thinking and being. The value of those lessons became apparent when I was asked to give a humorous keynote talk about the impact of digital technology on business communications.

The keynote talk was to be given at a national conference for senior executives. My Type A audience was attending so they could *embrace* and sell all things technology. I knew I was different than the typical conference attendee. So I needed a *hook* that would allow me to present business-communication challenges in a fresh, entertaining way. While I didn't care how much they liked their gadgets, I did want to present myself in an authentic manner that would bring the audience together no matter what their profession, industry, cultural background, or gender.

I held multiple meetings with myself asking questions like: "What the heck am I going to say to these people?" I must have held too many of these sessions, because my inner voice started to respond with a full-on Queens' irritated tone.

That's when I started to realize that Queens had not only given me my unique speaking voice, but it had also influenced my interpersonal style. Somewhere in the process of coexisting with a multitude of characters and nationalities, and navigating my way around a borough that never made sense, I had actually learned something about communicating with people and developing authentic relationships.

I fashioned those insights into *The Learned-it-in-Queens Communications Playbook*, a book that teaches *Winning against Digital Distraction*. My simple goal was to keep it *real* to get results.

In this book, you will find a humorous explanation of life in Queens that will teach you how to be an insider. Then I'll share an overview of current communication-mutant challenges and their accompanying opportunities. And finally, we will get to my eight practical plays that can help you be a *bettah* communicator—Queens style.

# Dedication

To my husband, Joe, and all the other people who have helped shape my life.

And a special shout out to Queens, the borough that made me who I am, and to NYC, a city that never quits.

*This is the corner closest to my old house. We could call it my Queens' starting point. Always remember where you came from.*

Photo by Julienne Ryan

# Introduction

## So what's the point of this book, and why should you keep reading?

No matter what you do or where you live, you're going to have to spend time communicating with another living human being. Chances are, you will use text, instant messages, email, or the next newest virtual thing. These can become digital distractions. However, your interactions may even happen *in person*, and include *eye contact!* Sometimes, the person you are communicating with may be different than you, but if you are patient, and fortunate, you will learn something from that experience.

## Why does this even matter?

Because I said so! Ok, that's not a good response, but I couldn't resist saying it. Listen, our lives provide us with too many regular opportunities to overact or be angry. That is a de-energizing, counter-productive space in which to exist. Has anything or anyone ever really changed for the better when someone barked out, "What the heck is wrong with you?" We lose the communication game when we fall into that trap.

Having positive face-to-face interactions can leave us feeling connected, uplifted, enriched, and rejuvenated. They help us form relationships that allow us to be more productive. They also help our mental health. They keep us in a state of wellness.

## So what's this book's BIG IDEA?

There are simple things we can do that will help us communicate and get out of our own way! Just for you, I'm going to share some unforgettable pictures and common-sense insights about what we can do to make our lives and the lives of others better.

We have to remember that we all speak lots of different languages. If I am going to help you have a better life, you need to know that where I come from in Queens, the word "better" is pronounced *bettah*.

More importantly, I am going to suggest a few things that will help us stop and think before we say or do something stupid! Technology enables doing rash and senseless things. But, this playbook contains cutting edge techniques like, "How looking up and talking to another human can be a smart thing to do!" And, "How picking up the phone to have a living, breathing conversation can help you!"

Having this playbook will be like having my clone follow you around saying, "Hey! I am talking to you! Look up and listen to me. Pay attention!" Are these rules that I am about to share foolproof? Yes, but No! (NYC is a very litigious place as a whole. From the time we are school children, we are taught to include a legal disclaimer in every document we write. Legally speaking, "no" may be just as valid as "yes.")

You are going to have to do the heavy lifting, aka "the work" and adjust your mindset and behaviors. Come on! You know that there's no instant anything. If you really want to make a change, you have to practice and work on your skills!

## What's next?

You gotta read the book and keep it handy. What did you think I was going to say? Now let's turn a page and have some fun. Yes, learning is fun!

Thanks for reading,

*Julienne*

*"You know, I do speak the Queens English. It's just the wrong Queens that's all. It's over the 59th Street Bridge. It's not over the Atlantic Ocean."*

—Cyndi Lauper, singer, producer

# A Queensite Primer

## An important study aid

As a resident of Queens, you're a Queensite, which is pronounced Queens-ite. You will have an enhanced learning experience if you read this book with a real Queens, New York accent. So begin by learning some basic Queens' phonetics and expressions so you can pretend that you are having a conversation with me.

## A short introduction to the infamous Queens *er* and *ea* sounds

I spent most of my adult life trying to avoid saying words like "here's, there's and ideas."

But occasionally I would have to say these words out loud in conversations like, "Here's the deal, there's no way around it, my ideas are best." Now the way you read that, and the way I read that, probably are not the same.

The Queensite's pronunciation is ***"heere's, theaare's & ideeeas."*** When uttered at a certain pitch and volume, they have the ability to cut through concrete and can be brutal on the ears! However, these pronunciations do have the power of getting your attention.

| Common | Queensite | Explanation |
| --- | --- | --- |
| Forget about it! | *Fuhgetaboutit!* | Someone humbly dismissing the genius of his or her actions. |
| Did you know? | *Didjaknow?* | The speaker is sharing wisdom. Pay attention. |
| How did you get here? | *Howd yagethere?* | Not about your personal experience, but your route and what was working or running, i.e. bus. |
| What are you talking about? | *Whataya talkinabout?* | The listener is questioning your logic or sanity. |
| Are you kidding me? | *Are ya kiddinme?* | Something is nuts! |
| That's nothing! | *Dat's nuthin!* | A humble comment or a dismissal of your efforts. |
| Do you plan on finishing your meal? | *Ya gonna eat dat?* | I'll eat that if you won't. |

*NawdoyagitwhadI'mtalkinabout?*

*Getting the most out of your conversations is like parking a car in Queens. You better not tear off a bumper making your point.*

Photo by Julienne Ryan

# Living In Queens

First, let me explain what it was like to live in Queens so you understand where I'm coming from. You need some context if we are going to *communicate* here.

Queensites plan their daily lives like a military operation. There's no such thing as being *chilled out* and *rolling out the door.* To get anywhere in Queens is a hassle. Our relaxing trip is never going to happen. Leaving to go anywhere requires intense planning and a list of questions in an ongoing dialogue:

Is there anything going on with the subways or buses today?

Are there any strikes, protests, festivals, marches, marathons, international-heads-of-state arrivals, major-sport events, fashion-week events, weather conditions, construction projects, or unforeseen circumstances that will prevent us from crossing over, entering, or reaching our destination?

Can we travel across the island of Manhattan the same day we leave Queens?

How long do you think it will take us to get there?

A query of any of these questions is always accompanied by a heated, 15-minute discussion and nobody talking to anyone else for the next 45 minutes, in other words, until we get to the next light.

When we are seized with a masochistic desire to drive, it's important to ask these next questions.

What's it look like outside? Is the pothole-to-street-surface ratio still navigable with something less than an armored tank?

And Queensite drivers need to know if there is any chance we can find legal, street parking nearby and that our car will still be there when we get back. "Parking nearby" means that we have found a cross-our-fingers-and-hope-that-it-really-is legal parking space that is only four, long blocks away.

The responses to any of the aforementioned questions are usually questions themselves: "*Whadaya kiddinme?*" And, "*Whereduyathink* we live? Montana?" (A documented Queens' native fact: When a Queensite's life passes in front of his or her eyes, 80% is devoted to the commute.)

However, Queensites are ever the unflaggingly, deluded optimists. We leave home every day with the hope that today will actually be a good commuting day. With that said, we do maintain a very low bar of what constitutes a good commute.

Pragmatic by nature, we also pack for commuting survival. We schlep (a Yiddish word that everyone uses that means "carry stuff") spare shoes, phone chargers, food and water, medicine, first aid kits, a miniature salon and spa of self-care products, tools, books, laptops, other assorted items of must-haves, and umbrellas and hats, "because we never know if those weather people got it right."

## Why is this the case?

Queensites don't get anywhere without doing a lot of walking, running, standing, and stair climbing. We've got to if we are going to get through or out of the borough. But we spend the most time *waiting* for *any kind* of functioning transportation to show up. When something actually shows up, chances are it will break down as soon as we get on it. So you can see why Queensites have no choice but to develop excellent coping skills. We always have to have a *Plan B* in place!

Waiting takes up a good part of our waking existence, so much so that it becomes part of our greetings. No cheery "hellos" or "good mornings" for us. No, it's more like "*Didjaknow* how long it took me to get in this morning?"

"You took two hours to go two subways stops? Dat's nothing! It took me three hours this morning and most of the time we were traveling backwards and in the dark!"

It's worth noting, Queensites are great complainers and will engage in competitive rounds of "problem poker" (my expression that describes competitive complaining).

As a result, one of the givens of Queens' life is that we have plenty of time, and I mean *plenty* to have a conversation, philosophize or sleep on the transportation—if we're lucky enough to get a seat. We can even create our own personal learning program. In my case, I spent my time listening to and watching other people. So now you know a thing or two about living in Queens.

*Theoretically, you can get from here to there...eventually*

Map by NYC.gov and stylized by Chad Spader

# Good Luck Getting There

Like I have been saying, living in Queens made me and the rest of my fellow Queensites scrappy and resilient. We always had to try harder to earn respect and recognition. In order to fully appreciate that comment, you need to understand a few things about how New Yorkers view each other's boroughs. You may not know this, but there is an inter-borough hierarchy.

First, there's Manhattan, of course. Everyone in the world knows about that place. It's fancy; it's famous, and everyone wants to go there. Then there's Brooklyn and The Bronx. TV shows and movies have helped create their reputations. These two boroughs have always fought it out for second place. However, nowadays Brooklyn has become cool, so they are winning at the moment.

That leaves Queens and Staten Island to duke it out for the next spot. Let's be honest. No one ever visits Staten Island unless they have relatives there or are trying to get to Jersey, so Queens definitely beats them out. Queensites feel like winners.

The more I think about Queens, the more it occurs to me that the borough is a pretty good analogy for what happens when we communicate. It's especially true when it comes to our digital communications.

## Navigating through the borough of Queens and cyberspace have a lot in common!

First of all, Queens is a dynamic, diverse borough of 2.3 million people. Almost half (48%) are foreign born, speaking over 800 languages. That's a lot of diversity, complexity, coexisting happening in an area that's only 109 square miles.

You might say that it looks something like the jumble of radio, television, and wireless phone signals that course through, above, and around our country.

The second reason why Queens reminds me of our digital communications and cyberspace is that Queensites get lost a lot. It's like a dropped call or a lost voice mail. We don't understand how to get around our borough. No one *really* does!

You see, our borough started off as series of farming villages that got smooshed together as the borough's population grew. Take a look at the map of Queens.

To put it mildly, the place is confusing. Roads stop, reappear, and repeat without any visible logic. You have names like 32nd Street, 32nd Avenue, and 32nd Court. Many of them exist right next to each other. They abruptly stop just before you get to the place you were going. They reappear again miles away. And, oh, if you are looking for the crossroads from hell, you have come to the right place.

In the days before GPS, I'd find myself and my fellow Queensites walking around looking like a bunch of wilderness trackers as we tried to figure out how to get from one point to another.

Spending our formative years getting lost and trying to figure stuff out takes an emotional toll. All of that confusion and frustration, leaves its mark. It shaped our personalities and impacted how we dealt with the world. Queensites end up becoming what civilized people call "a bit quirky."

Our borough has created some unique characters. No doubt about it! Here are some examples of people who came from Queens:

- Awkwafina
- LL Cool J
- RodneyDangerfield
- Cyndi Lauper
- John Leguizamo
- Nicky Minaj
- Donald Trump
- Christopher Walken
- Mae West

So like any Queensite trying to navigate their borough on any given day, you and I spend a lot of time dealing with our digital and in-person communication challenges. Digital distraction forces us to develop our unique, scrappy resilience. We ask ourselves, "How do I authentically communicate in a complex world?"

*I am listening. Are you for real?*

Photo by Bicanski from Pixnio

# Be Alert

My research for this book began in primary school. As a Queens' kid, I took New York City buses and trains, not regular school buses to get to school. I spent a lot of time coming in contact with strangers. So naturally, my parents gave me conflicting guidance to help me navigate my daily commutes and to safely cope with my environment.

"Be aware of your surrounding at all times."

"Know who's standing near you."

"But don't look or stare at strangers."

Huh? How's that supposed to work?

I figured out a way to follow these rules by developing extraordinary peripheral, aka, *bird's eye* scanning capabilities (like the pigeon on the previous page). I was able to look at people without getting *caught*. Not only did I want to know who was near me, I wanted to check out what people were wearing, reading, or talking about, because a NYC commute is *live theatre* every day.

I got really good at checking out people without them noticing that I was studying them. I would feign interest in the English and Spanish subway/bus ads. Not only did I watch people, I learned a foreign language. While I was always challenged in high school French Class, I learned how to say in Spanish "don't lean or hold the subway doors" and "pull this cord in an emergency" with great confidence. Those learning habits enabled me to operate in a state of *commuter readiness* while managing my commuting boredom and never-ending teenage frustration.

*Digitally distracted NYC Subway riders fill the cars. We've grown a species of heads-down people.*

Photo from Shutterstock

# PeopleHaveMutated!

## They have turned themselves into a "Heads-Down, Living-in-a-Bubble Species!"

My secret people-scanning skills have served me well my entire life. However, a few years ago I realized that peoplewatching was becoming way too easy. I no longer needed my super-stealth competitive edge. People have changed. *Nobody is looking up anymore.*

People who once walked with their heads held up high have been infected with digital distraction. They have mutated. Their chins are now fixed to their chests. Their eyes follow the alluring electronic, never-ending scroll.

Check out our current subway scene. The minions are looking at their devices or talking to people who aren't with them. Nobody seems to be looking around at their surroundings or day dreaming. They are certainly not paying attention to the stranger next to them. *Creatures from outer space* could be gripping the overhead bar trying to keep their balance on the jerky, earthly ride, and our mutants wouldn't even notice it.

When I discovered this, I really started to listen-in on conversations. Yes, I eavesdrop. You may call me over-curious or nosy. I call it *doing research*.

What did I hear?

**Big Surprise!**

I heard a lot of complaining about communications. One of the things I heard people talk about the most was that somebody, somewhere, wasn't getting back to them!

The more I listened to other people's conversations, the more it sounded like an endless loop of repetitive complaints:

No response! Why no response?

That person can't be gone, gone, gone!

I am just trying to get a response!

Why can't they just call me?

How many ways do I need to send messages so that one of them will actually get read, and I'll get a response?"

Then there were countless comments about who said what? Who didn't say something? Who said the wrong thing to the wrong person? Who never says anything? Who never bothers to call? Who did call but used the wrong tone?

Then it was all about who didn't look at them? Who was looking at them? Who was looking at them the wrong way? Who do they *wish* would look at them?

No matter where I went, the complaining was always there. It never stopped! The ironic thing was no matter who the people were, where they came from, their ages, their backgrounds, or even what they did for a living, they all agreed on one thing:

*We are all making each other a little crazy with the way we communicate*!

Sometimes that felt like the only thing people could agree on. Did I ever hear anyone say:

"Please give me more frustrating moments like this?"

No, of course not! So what are we doing to each other?

But wait a minute! Let me not get all Queens-girl, NewYork-City presumptuous on you. I don't want to assume that your experiences are the same as mine.

Maybe things are going better where you live. Maybe everyone is getting back to you. Maybe people understand everything you are trying to say when you send a message. Even better, you've got it all together, and you never experience interpersonal conflict!

For real? *Right.* I'm not buying it! You *bettah* keep reading this playbook!

*Our emails and texts are screaming for our attention.*

Photo from Shutterstock

# Our Messages Are in Hot Pursuit

Most of us try to behave like reasonable people *most of the time*, but we live in a world where information is being shared constantly. We're sending and receiving emails. Friends and colleagues are constantly posting and forwarding messages via Facebook, texts, Messenger, LinkedIn, etc. etc.

As an example, take yourself right now. You're reading this paragraph, and that makes me very happy. But while you're focusing on reading this playbook, you're probably frustrating someone out there in cyberspace! They are expecting something from you.

When I think about our cyber messages, I visualize them like the gargoyles in the old Ghostbuster movies (or like in this royalty-free, and oh-so-much-cheaper visual example). They're coming to life and flinging themselves through cyberspace trying to reach us. Things start buzzing, vibrating, ringing, and pinging. It is an unrelenting pursuit. It never stops. The spirits of the e-message churn up the sender and twist the receiver's emotions!

We are rarely totally engaged or present. We are digitally distracted. And as I said earlier, on an ongoing basis we have tuned out what's happening around us.

Now it's challenging enough if the person who is trying to reach you knows you, or has some context about why you may not be responding. They may know you are out of the office. Perhaps they know you are hiding somewhere and reading your new favorite book! Or maybe they are aware that you never respond to messages that you don't like. But what happens if the person you either accidentally, or intentionally, are not responding to is from a different generation or background? What happens if they have different cultural expectations of what constitutes good or appropriate communications?

Worse, what happens if this is how they *always* experience you? Do they feel totally "dissed" (slang expression that every Queensite knows that means disrespected) or even incensed?

Many of us are so focused on our personal "getting it done" we aren't aware of the dynamic we are creating. The e-spirits are constantly coming to life, and if we are not careful, we are going to get slimed!

Ironically, we are simultaneously *perpetrators and sufferers of digital distractions, cyber mistreatments, and electronic mishaps!* We are giving as good as we get whether we know it or not.

Go ahead and admit it. Our messages are in hot pursuit.

*So that's what you think?*

Visual by Chad Spader, photo from Shutterstock

# What Did You Say?

Ibrought my big Code-Red Angry Dude along for back up so I could make sure that you were paying attention.

Most of us get *frustrated* and sometimes angry when we don't hear back from someone. When we finally do get a response, many times we don't like or understand it!

Then we find ourselves turning into our own version of the big Code-Red Angry Dude. When we are upset, it's easy to overreact!

How many times are we tempted to respond right away and just *let it all out*? But does reacting this way help?

Has *losing it* ever solved our difficulties? Probably not. Here's a question to ask yourself the next time you get a message you don't like and want to reply immediately with something less than civility.

Am I really reading the actual message or is something else going on?

This question can help, because maybe the situation isn't actually how it appears to you in the moment. But one thing is for sure. If you let loose with a rip-roaring, angry response, things will certainly go from bad to worse!

## What helps us in these Code-Red situations?

First of all, when you are in the middle of a communication that's hitting your buttons, remember the image of the Code-Red Angry Dude that you would rather not become, then hit your internal *pause* button.

Next, do nothing! Send nothing! Call nobody until you've given yourself a chance to settle down.

Got it? Good!

OK, I'm hitting my internal *pause* button.

You see, when you overreact, there is a very good chance that you're going to make a very *big mistake.* When that happens, you are going to wish you could have a *do-over* with a fresh start. But sometimes you don't get another chance.

For the record, though, *do-over* is a time-honored, Queensite request for a break. For kids, if granted in a game, it allows you to repeat a play or a turn. It's reserved for those crucial times when you've thrown the frisbee over a neighbor's fence or a softball through the neighbor's front window. For adults, it's reserved for those crucial times when you've put *your foot in your mouth.* Did I just say that *out loud?* Do-over please!

So hit the internal *pause* button and remember the CodeRed Angry Dude, which is never your best look.

Let's keep moving, so we can find out about what happens in our brains when we are communicating.

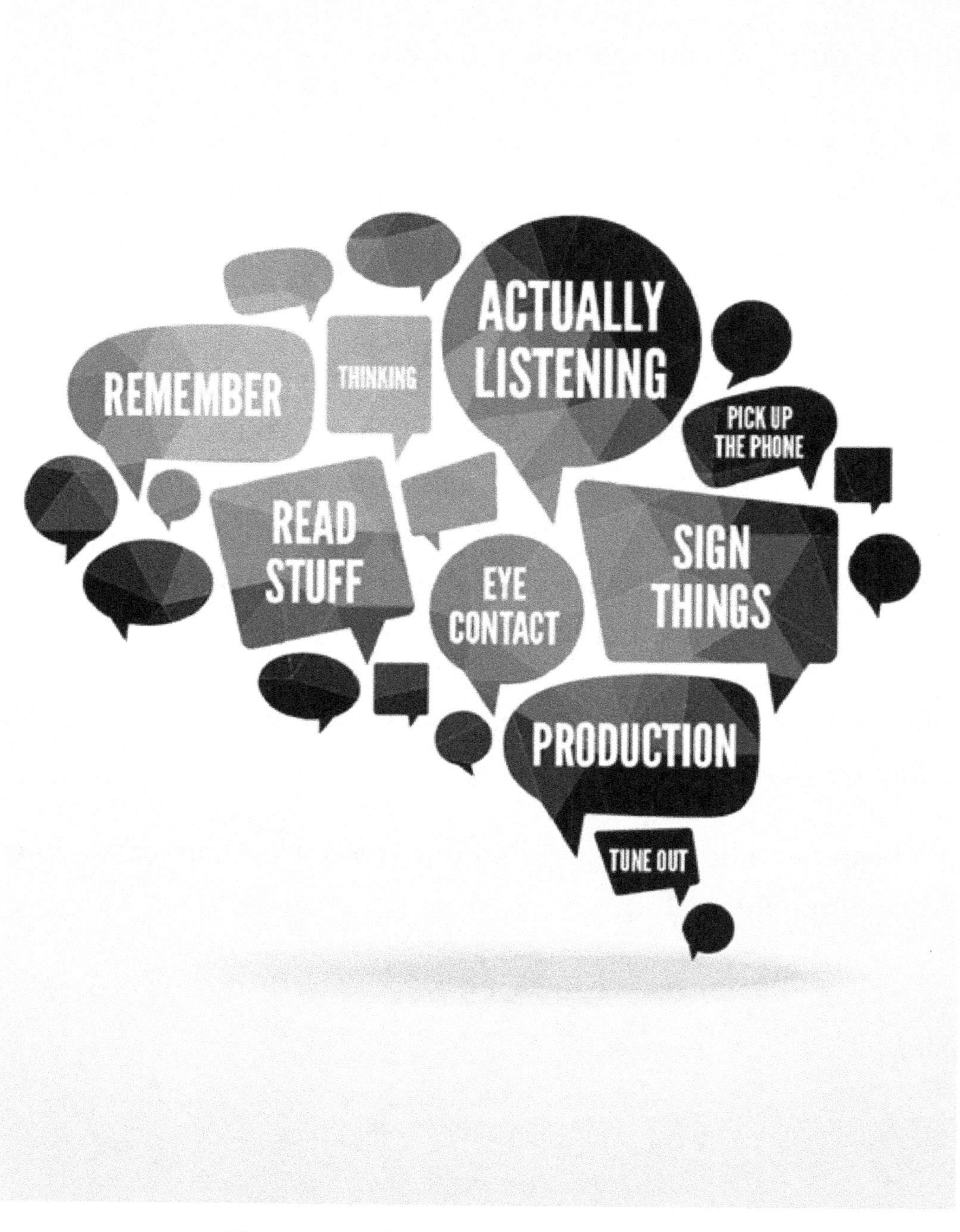


*This is what's bubbling up inside our brains.*

Visual by Chad Spader

# Our Brain at Work and my *Very* Scientific Explanation

## What's going on in our brains when we are communicating?

Ok, I got only *one thing to say here*, so listen up. When we communicate, we are making the assumption that we are actually getting into the part of the other person's brain that we need and want: the actually-listening part. We expect that the other person looks up from his or her device and takes notice of what we are saying. Our brain thinks their brain is going to remember this interchange!

But this communication assumption is like the street hucksters you run into in New York neighborhoods. Those guys sell handbags, watches, and phone accessories and try to convince you that their goods are the *real thing* and that they are giving you a *real deal*. Well, most of the time, they're not.

## Our ASSUMPTIONS are trouble makers.

Our *successful-communication* ASSUMPTION tries to sell us a bunch of stuff that ain't real. It says:

Of course, my message was read.

Yes, I am sure they listened to my voice mail.

They probably dropped everything they were doing to think about my request.

Obviously that person I am trying to contact still works at the company.

I am sure they realized that when I sent them a holiday greetings card, they were supposed to immediately go and talk to their boss about doing business with me.

Yes, they *understood* my email and knew *exactly* what they were s*upposed* to do next!

That last one is my favorite! But wait a minute; I am picking up on your vibes. You don't believe that this is the way your brain works? You want me to prove it with data?

**Ok, I get it. I question everything I read, too.**

But *areyakiddingme?* This is me you're talking to! Of course, I could have included a ton of impersonal, data-riddled graphs and wordy citations on every page. I could have selected imposing font and not included pictures! I could have named dropped, and referenced my education or who I know. But would that have made you pay better attention or change *anything* you were doing? No? So I didn't.

STOP QUESTIONING WHAT I WROTE AND PAY ATTENTION.

Actually, you make a good point, though. I need to be listening here, too. After all, this is a communications playbook. Do you know why I know what I say is true?

## I *do have data* and lots of it!

The New York City metropolitan area has 8.5 million residents, *and* that's not including all the suburban and out-of-state commuters from Connecticut, New Jersey, and parts of Pennsylvania. These people show up for work every day in New York City. (True New Yorkers say "we are going into The City." We never say "New." When you visit our city and say the whole name, we know immediately that you are from out of town. Just saying!)

Oh, and here's another big data point. Consider the ton of tourists and business travelers who roam our streets on a daily and nightly basis.

Those are the *data pools* I have seen exhibiting my findings. I have been observing a lot of people not looking up, walking around in their bubble of assumptions, and in general, being digitally distracted.

Now I know from the tortuous statistics classes I had to take in school that *8.5 million people, plus a ton of other people* represents a *statistical relevant cohort!* So there! My findings are data driven. This is *very* scientific stuff.

We are going to use the findings of this data as a thinking prompt. We've got to answer the following question about our communications:

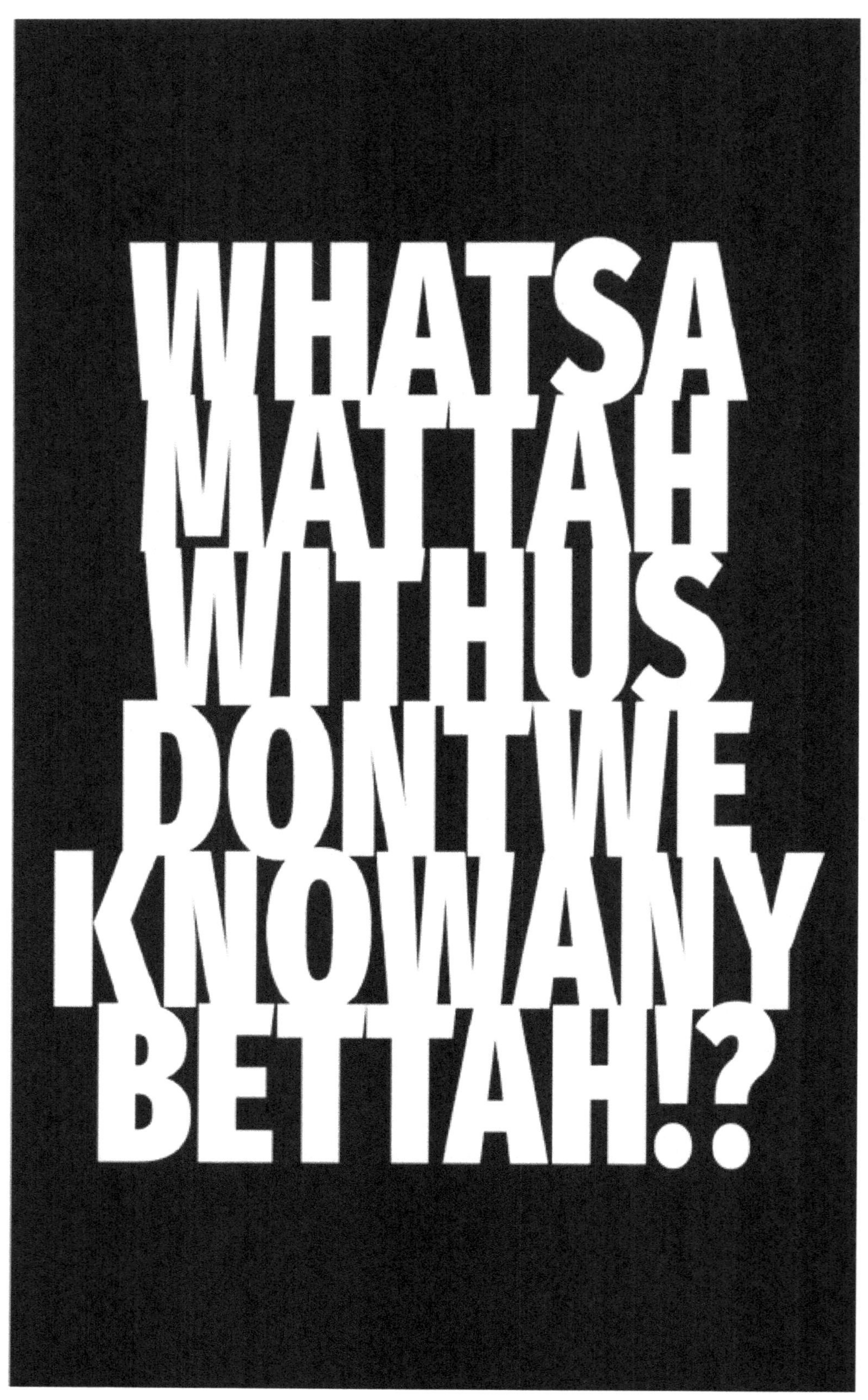


Visual by Chad Spader

# Here's what I think

I believe that you are a smart, curious person. Otherwise you wouldn't have started reading this playbook. You don't need me to create a huge academic study so I can tell you that it may be a good idea *to look up once a while, pause, and pay attention to how we are communicating!*

Just about everybody knows there are special problems communicating today. We want to be *understood* and to *understand*. It is time to share the learned-it-in-Queens plays that will help you win against digital distraction.

So here I go with my first Learned-it-in-Queens Playbook Lesson!

*Serve up your genuine, authentic sauce, I mean, self!*

Photo by Chad Spader

# Play #1 — Keep It Authentic

**W**e need to keep it authentic! If you want to win against digital distraction, you have to communicate authentically. But not only do we need to be authentic, most of us need to figure out how to keep it together on any given day!

**Let me explain with a slice of New York pizza.**

When Queensites eat a slice, we fold it in half so we don't lose any of the toppings, and we stop the olive oil and sauce from dripping all over us. We need to keep that slice together. We eat our pizza standing up, wedged around a little table, or walking down a street while we are talking. It's as simple as that.

It's the same way with our communications. We have got to figure out how to keep it together when we are authentically communicating. I totally get it how challenging that can be.

Communication is especially messy when you realize that you have just left your 32nd message and have figured out 20 new ways to say, "I am circling back to you yet again!"

It's hard not to want to lose it when the message isn't getting through! But you can't lose it. You have to figure out a way to keep it together like you do when you're eating a slice. You don't want to wear your miscommunication all over the front of your nice white shirt.

Try to remember who you are and what you were trying to accomplish before you left all those messages. What kind of image do you want to project?

**Keep it authentic and keep it together.**

*The elevated Flushing, Queens # 7 line. We'll be coming 'round the corner... Arriving, maybe soon.*

Photo from Shutterstock

# Play #2 — When Stuck, Try Something New

Sometimes you can't get from here to there. Some days you can't get anywhere! Our communications get stuck just like a stalled train.

For example, take the #7 Flushing Line Train. Well, the train's service has been so bad that my friend Melissa created the *7 Train Blues Blog* and a commuter advocacy group called *Access Queens*. Melissa did this while she was stuck on this train. *Yes, she had that much spare time!* She formed the group based on a radical vision that the train should move and actually take passengers somewhere!

Sometimes, our communications are like those #7 Flushing Trains. They are going nowhere. They're "dead in their tracks."

No reply. Nothing. No one is picking up the phone. Are they really out for lunch at 9:47 a.m.?

Then there's our email experiences. How many times have you have sent out a simple, brief email only to discover a minute later that your inbox has just doubled in size? Your email inbox chain is "lighting up!"

That inbox is not full of supportive, enthusiastic responses or innovative ideas. Your message has been stopped in its tracks. Most of those responses are from people who have been "cc'd." They are reading the messages out of context!

Suddenly there's on-line shouting going on, because the emailing horde has decided that they have to opine. There are those people who write something because they always have to put in their two-cents worth no matter what the topic is, even if they don't know anything about it! Then there is the person who saw that the other people wrote something and decided, "Well, I better weigh in, too."

Next, there are the people who are isolated and working from home. They want to be focused and actually get something done, but they have gotten distracted because their instant messenger has been pinging constantly for five minutes. They respond so they can show their team that they are really working and are not goofing off.

As you read your email stream, you can feel the energy being sucked out of the universe. Suddenly everyone is taking sides; nothing is getting accomplished or solved. Your communications are stuck. Things are going from bad to worse. You may never get off the #7 Flushing train!

When I wrote this section, I shared these email scenarios with Carol, a successful business owner. She responded, "Oh my god, you are describing a situation we encountered at our company!"

She went on to share, "My firm had been working with a very good client for a long time. Suddenly the relationship shifted. We'd send out a beautiful, well-constructed email and then we'd receive back a testy response. We'd craft another thoughtful email only to get the same reaction again. It was getting bad. I was getting worried because this client represented a substantial part of our revenue."

## "What did you do?" I asked.

Carol replied, "I knew something was not right. I knew that our account was in jeopardy if we did not take action and solve the communications problem. So I picked up the phone and called the client to arrange for a meeting. Do you know what was causing the problem? Firewalls. Our messages to a long-standing customer were getting blocked, because the client had upgraded their firewalls. Our questions were being read out of context because the majority of our emails had never arrived. Frankly, our client had thought that we had lost our collective smarts and skills."

So there you go; the technology that was designed to protect the communication between two companies was causing it to fail. More emails would not solve the issue. Sometimes you can't get anywhere unless you get on a new train. The previous one is stuck in place and may even slide backwards. Fortunately, this business owner had the good sense to listen to her gut, and take action.

## What will you do when this happens to you?

I recommend following Carol's approach. When you're getting nowhere, or when your communications are causing problems, try something new. Set up a face-to-face meeting or a call. Chances are there's more to your message exchange than you realize. Go live, and help both sides *save face*. Pick up the phone, write an old-fashioned letter, text rather than email, send a pigeon, but do *something* to disrupt the negative dynamic!

*Soooo, you haven't answered my message.*

Photo from Shutterstock

# Play #3 — Hey, Take A Breath

Communicating can be stressful. It's important to learn coping skills that will help you at work and at home. You're probably thinking, "If she tells me to take a moment to breathe and meditate, I am throwing this playbook out the window!"

I'm with you.

There is nothing more annoying than having someone tell you to "chill out" when you're aggravated. I'm going to let you in on a little secret about Queensites and New Yorkers in general. Never, ever tell us to "just relax" when we are going through something. Those words make us even crazier! No joke. I am just sharing this wisdom in case you're thinking about coming to our city, or some of your Queens relatives are scheduling a visit to your house. Be careful what you say.

Listen, I don't have anything against mindful meditation. I have practiced it. Breathe in. Breathe out. Breathe in. Ok I'm done. Well, let me ask you this? While I was busy doing all those lengthy inhalations did anyone bother getting back to me? No! So what was the point of all that heavy breathing? I could have been doing something else with my time!

All I'm saying here is that you have to find a positive coping technique that works for you. So now, I am going to share what does work for me, but you have to promise me that you are going to keep it just between us.

Come closer. Go ahead, promise it, but you bettah promise it in a whisper.

What do I do when my communications are not going as planned? I visualize myself as lead character in an old-school, good-fella type movie. Yes, you read that correctly. Envision this, a short, blonde, middle-aged female, me, sits at my desk and leans back in my black, ergonomic chair. I check my emails. No response.

Next, I check the phone. No new voice mail messages. Not a single one!

Perhaps that person sent me a text? Nada! (Spanish for "Nothing.")

Basta! (Italian for "That's enough!")

My coping skills fully kick in. I say, "That's it. You're dead to me! *Fuhgetaboutit*!!!"

Then I feel a lot better. I can move on. That's how I take my *meditative* breath. Now I can do something productive and proactive.

But let's step away from that analogy and try not to dwell too much on how my brain works. Instead, let's focus on what happens when reasonable, well-functioning people like yourself don't get or give the response they desire.

Find something that will calm you down. I am listing a few ideas here to prime your pump, but remember, you are the one who has to actually do the work, so pick wisely.

- **"Start writing your lines"** was what my grade school nun used to say to her unruly class. That would quiet the room! Suddenly the whole class would have their heads bent down over their notebooks writing furiously, "I promise that I will not talk in class." We would write that 100 times in long-hand script! There is something meditative about it. You could try writing, "I will not call or email anyone until I have reigned in my emotions." Perhaps writing that just a dozen times might help.

- **Get up and move.** When you feel like you're about to explode, no good can come of communicating with that unfettered emotion churning inside of you. So get moving! Walk, jump up and down, or shimmy and shake yourself about for no less than 20 minutes for the full cardio effect, but even 20 seconds can make a difference in your attitude.

- **Convert your emotion into a donation**. Use your animated, heated, or impassioned emotion for good by fueling a worthy cause. One year, I contributed to an organization that provided farm animals to disadvantaged farmers overseas. By the end of that year, I had donated a small herd of goats to those in need. I even named one of the goats after the Queens girl writing this book. Seriously, focusing on doing good for others is a sure way of letting go of our own frustration and pain.

- **Maintain a chore drawer.** Dedicate a plastic bin or drawer to *micro mini projects* that you can work on when you are frustrated, impatient, or distracted. Sew a button back on your shirt. Write a thank you note to someone who did you a kindness. Untangle the chain of a necklace. Glue back together a broken ceramic piece. In other words, focus your attention on a small positive task.

- **Take a moment to laugh or smile.** Watching silly-animal and other comedy videos can help you regroup. Take your mind off of your troubles with some mindless entertainment. Or check out old-school Queens' talent like Cindy Lauper or Rodney Dangerfield. Get your respect back!

*There is a lot of stuff that could come out of me at any moment!*

Visual by Chad Spader, photo by Shutterstock

# Play #4 — Hold on to Your Inner Child!

Our digital communication tools have helped us create a world where we are hanging out together 24/7. It's like we are kids in constant contact with our friends in this enormous cyberspace-school playground.* And just like it was when we were younger, there's always a couple of characters who are trying to stir things up.

Let's name the first group of those cyber characters *Assumptions*. You remember those, don't you? They like to gang up on us and make our lives miserable. Make no mistake about it. *Assumptions* are hanging out in all of our playgrounds. And sometimes they bring a tougher group called *Transference*.

Now when *Assumptions* and *Transference* get together, they like nothing better than to mess with our heads to get us to do something stupid. They like to taunt our *inner child*.

So they sidle up to us and start whispering in our ears so they can start some trouble. Now, if we have had a good experience with someone or a group, the trouble we get into might not be so bad. *Assumptions* and *Transference* might make us think, "Oh, people like me. It is just like it was in third grade. Isn't life great? Everyone is going to return my note right away."

"Hmm, maybe they will, but maybe they won't." Either way, those potentially troubling thoughts have a habit of finding a way to sneak into your head.

And another thing, what happens when you have had a negative experience (in the past) with someone like your colleague, teacher, recruiter, or potential client? When that happens, it is best for you to be on high alert and watch out! Let's say that you have been working on a project and have been trying to reach person X so he can help you. He is supposed to do something important or provide essential information. You thought you made it clear that this is a time-sensitive situation, but you haven't heard back from him as promised.

*Assumptions* and *Transference* are eager to jump in and *help you*. They come over to you and start whispering in your ear. They're not just talking to intelligent, mature you. They are also *egging on* your *inner child.* *Assumptions* will make you say, "He got my message. He knows what I have requested. He's fully aware of the timeline."

*Transference* gets you to think, "Good luck with getting that person to call me! He's just like that teacher I had in school that never liked me and always gave me a hard time! He's not getting back to me on purpose. He's never going to do right by me. He's acting like this so he can make me look bad."

Now to your credit, you have managed to stay cool and rational up to this point, well barely. Then you decide to take a break and check some of your social media feeds. Suddenly you see that the person who told you, "I'm so busy that I can't get back to you" has been tweeting and blogging about life. He's even shared his favorite shopping site!

You start to think to yourself, "Well, how come he has time to write and connect with others, but he doesn't have time for me?"

Really! Is this really happening?

Warning! Now's the time to hang on to your *inner child.* Because s/he is about to get loose, and s/he doesn't want to act like an adult with a communications playbook in hand.

That kid inside of us really moves fast! It's trying to pull away from your adult grasp. S/he wants to scream at the colleague you need help from and say, "Yo! I am talking to you! What's your problem?"

We have got to hold on tight, and distract the *inner children* and stop them before they break loose and start something that's destined to go badly!

Here's one thing for sure. Because we're each working in a digital communication bubble, our in-person contact is limited, even when we are sitting a few seats away from our colleagues.

As they receive our messages and respond to us, we don't see their facial expressions and don't have the benefit of hearing their voices and their vocal tone. As a result, we lack the visual and auditory cues that provide important nuances. As a result, our communications are running amuck.

We cannot let our *inner children* take over our work and life. We have to make sure that we are not falling victim to *Assumptions* and *Transference.* We need strategy to win against digital distraction.

## Our Thoughts Are Not Reality

So what are we going to do the next time we see that *Assumptions* and *Transference* are stirring up trouble, trying to make us run amuck?

First, we need to spot them. Then block them. And finally stop them.

Remind ourselves that *Assumptions* and *Transference* are only too happy to get us angry and impatient. When we feel angry or impatient, we need to ask ourselves: Why?

Before we jump to conclusions, we do well to remember that *our thoughts are not reality*.

Being immersed in digital communication, we have an abundance of opportunities to jump to conclusions when we are reading or listening to messages. We take this information in, but it is not the full picture of life. It is just ones and zeros. That's why we call it digital. Just those two digits infinitely arranged and creatively transposed.

We write these virtual make-believe scripts in our head. We assemble our own thoughts on what we have received. Our thoughts may be our personal truths, and our best guesses, but they are not always correct.

So the next time an email exchange, phone conversation, or video conference starts to heat up remember: Hold on to that *inner child* and don't let *Assumptions* and *Transference* spoil your day.

*It was me. It was me. It was all me. I was wrong.*

Visual by Chad Spader, photo by Shutterstock

# Play #5 — Admit it, Sometimes You Get It Wrong

Sometimes we get it wrong. These are not easy words for me to write, because I know that I don't want to be labeled:

"The Person Who Messed Up!"

I realized a long time ago that no one in Queens is perfect. Queensites make mistakes, and they usually come clean about it. "My bad," is something you can hear almost every day.

In the digital communications world, where we are all distracted, all of us are guilty of simple but impactful mistakes. We might not have checked our messages and then blamed someone else for having a hidden issue or not following through. Yes, people are going to have issues, but sometimes we have to face facts. We need to be honest when we realize that the miscommunication was our fault.

We missed that last message in the email train.

Or perhaps this scenario has happened to you? You communicated a message, but a bit later you can't remember what tool you used to send it? You ask yourself:

"Did I send a message via LinkedIn or was it an email? Was it a text or was it a live conversation? Did I actually talk to them on the phone?"

Then you have an insight. You start to piece the parts together as you continue your internal monologue:

"Wait a minute. I remember coming up with a lot of good ideas, and organizing them into bullet points. Bullet points? That's definitely a clue. Why do I remember bullets? It must have been an email. Yes, I remember thinking that it was a very good one. No, it was better than good. That email was practically a work of art! It had all the great elements of humor, thoughtful wisdom, and actionable suggestions! Now I am really getting annoyed because this email was not accorded the respect and the prompt attention it deserved!"

So if you're like me, you shoot off an, oh-so-polite email asking when your recipients would like to respond to your incredible email.

But then you experience a full-body jolt as you read this reply:

"No, we never saw an email from you."

You think, "*Areyakiddinme*?"

But hang on a minute. The thought train just pulled into the station. You ask:

"Why does my draft folder have a red number #1 on it? OMG, the email has been stuck in my drafts! It never went anywhere!"

All that artistic wisdom of that email was like a pigeon perched on a cable wire. It was just sitting there waiting to fly away.

Now I have to face the cold hard facts of the city. They didn't mess up. It was me!

**What is the best thing to do when this happens?**

Well, if we want to be viewed as authentic and trustworthy individuals, we have to demonstrate a little courage. As we say in Queens, I've got to "Deal with it!"

We have to honestly own up to our mistakes, privately (one-to-one email), and publicly (group email).

To get the competitive edge on digital distraction, this is a huge opportunity. It's so simple. We've got to *man and woman up* and say those magic words:

"I am sorry. It was my mistake!"

*Let's sit down together and get real.*

Photo with my friend Ronnie Rochester by Lava Semper

# Play #6 — Find *Your* Front Stoop

I know what you're thinking at this point.

"Hey! Enough with all this talk about what we are doing wrong and what we need to be thinking about! How about giving us some tips about things that will help us communicate?"

Let me just say to you:

"*Whatdyathink* I was going to leave you hanging?"

Here is one very important thing that will help. Find your version of a Queens' front stoop. (Front stoops are used for gathering places, where people sit, chat, and people watch. Oh, if you happen to walk by people sitting on their stoop, you better believe those people are going to look you over and talk about you.)

Go get the person you want to speak to and bring them to your front stoop. Sit next to them, look up at them, and listen!

"What did that Queens Girl just tell me to do? Go find a stoop? What the heck is she talking about?"

Well, you're not the first person to say that to me; so we're cool. When I was first writing the speech that prompted this book, I practiced my presentation in front of some very patient friends. (There is a special place in heaven waiting for anyone who has ever had to sit through one of my practice sessions.)

When I got to this part, my friend Martha interrupted me and asked, "Jules, are you sure that people are going to know what a 'stoop' is?"

To which I very patiently replied, *"Whatayatalkinabout?* What's so hard to understand? I am presenting to a smart group of people with big titles, and I am showing them a picture of people sitting on steps in front of their house. How hard is it going to be for them to understand that 'stoop' is a word for steps?"

To which Martha replied, "Just tell them!"

Ok, so here's a brief lesson about why Queens people (and other New Yorkers) call their front steps "stoops."

First, the Native Americans lived in the borough we now call Queens. Then the Dutch showed up and they had a habit of building very high steps in front of their homes just in case their neighborhood flooded. The Dutch word for those steps was "stoop." Then the British showed up and stayed for a good bit. Finally, the Brits left, and we became America, and then Queensites. Now fast forward to today! Although our city is known for its fast pace and constant change, the one thing we managed to keep for a few hundred years is the word "stoop." So now you know. Today's history lesson is done!

At the beginning of this playbook I had engaged in some old-fashioned Queensite name-calling and labeled us a *"heads-down people and a living-in-a-bubble species."*

I complained about this mutated trait of how we were not looking up anymore, or even engaging in conversations. I pointed out that we were over-reacting when we sent and received each other's messages.

So here's my pearl of wisdom. Of course, it starts with a question or two:

Do you have contact with *humans* every day, perhaps coworkers or other staff? Do you want to build productive relationships? Maybe you even want to spend less time with lawyers?

Find a stoop. Go live. Go human. Find your and their version of a front stoop. Find the places that you can go to sit side by side when you have a conversation. Then *listen* and have an *in-your-space* conversation, not an *in-your-face* interaction.

Practice *full-on focus*. Actively listen to the person next to you!

Doing this can make a difference. *Didjaknow* even if you only do it for a few minutes, it can have a lasting, positive effect? Well, now you know.

But don't think I can't hear you out there reacting and saying things like: "Get real! I live and work in a virtual world! I can't always meet with people in person!"

Ok. I understand. I get it, but I've got questions for you. Do you spend a lot of time on conference calls? Do you multi-task when you are on a conference call?

Come on, own up! I've bared my soul with you in this playbook. So be straight up and answer this question honestly! You multi-task, don't you? You do other stuff when you are talking to people virtually!

## That's what I thought. You need a virtual stoop.

Here's something to keep in mind the next time you are on an audio or video conference call and you let yourself become distracted. The person on the other end of the communication can sense that you are not really listening.

Yes, they can tell. Yes, this is a real thing. They know you're not all there. How do I know this?

I have spent many years interviewing, having meetings, and coaching by phone. I could always tell when the person on the other end of call was distracted and had *lost their connection* with me.

How do you tell when someone is distracted when they are not right in front of you? The *notes* in their voice are *off key*. The tone they use when they respond doesn't have the same depth and consistency. Simply put, their responses change when they are not *fully present*.

This happens when people try to speak to someone who is digitally distracted, as well. Pay attention the next time you are on a video conference call and you are sitting next to someone who has *checked out*. You can see that person is doing something else. They are digitally distracted.

Now listen carefully to the person's voice who *is speaking*. You'll hear his or her voice get a bit strained. They can sense that they have lost the connection with their listeners.

We humans are intuitive beings. We can tell when there has been a shift in energy. When you sit on the stoop you can tell when people are authentically present.

I don't want to be one of *those* people who don't really listen. And I want to help *my* people to not be one of *those* people, too. My Queensite guidance to myself (and you) is to practice *full-on focus* and *side-by-side, in-your-space* conversations.

Imagine you are sitting on the stoop next time you are on a conference call. Try it. See what happens when you make it a habit.

You might find your meetings and conversations shortening in length but improving in quality. *Use the power of small things to make a difference* in your communications and interactions. It's your *secret sauce* or your Sunday gravy, as we like to say in Queens. (This is what we call tomato with meat sauce.)

Practice the power of the *full-on focus* of the stoop to make a difference every day. It's life changing.

*Don't you listen bettah when your stomach is happy?*

Photo by Walt Pechulis, Jr.

# Play #7 — You Gotta Eat

A Queensite is never done speaking or eating! Other people you meet from the digitally distracted world also need to eat. You can use this information to your advantage.

You know how a Queensite gets to know you?

Food.

You know how we decide if you're friendship worthy? Food.

How do we show we like you? Food.

How do we build trust and understanding? Food.

Are you getting the message here? It's time to put this play into action with your work. Breaking bread together breaks down barriers. It nourishes relationships. It's the yeast of communication.

When things are important, we sit down for a meal. If a new group of people moves into the community from another part of the world, we share a meal together. You can do the same in your workplace.

How does a Queensite offer support and guidance when someone is encountering a life challenge? They utter these words: "You gotta eat! Then you'll figure things out!"

Our capacity to eat our people's food and everyone else's is probably why Queensites have done an amazing job of coexisting as not only the most diverse borough in New York but also the most diverse place in the United States.

We have a tasty wisdom that we use with new people, or any people for that matter. We get in a whole lot less trouble if our mouth is full of food. That way we have to spend some time listening while we are chewing.

When I have my childhood friend Kim over, there is a big discussion about what we should cook, what we are going to eat first, and what recipes we need to share and read. Food is on everyone's mind.

Here is the classic Queensite communication dilemma: What should we do first? Should we speak or eat? When the food arrives, it's a not even a contest. We're going to eat, of course! And speak very, very quickly in between mouthfuls!

If you have a communication dilemma at work, remember that food levels the playing field and solves many miscommunications.

I hate to finish this section. And now I'm starving.

*Ya gonna eat dat?*

*There's one more thing I gotta ask.*

Peter Falk as Columbo, publicity photo by Margie Korshak Associates

# Play #8 — Ask One More Question!

I promised you some great Learned-it-in-Queens Playbook insights. I believe that I have delivered on that promise. You have kept reading until the end, so I am going to give you one more communication play. It's a little something extra, and a very Queensite thing to do.

I am going to call on Columbo, one of my all-time favorite TV detectives to help me make my point. Columbo was played by New Yorker Peter Falk. Pretty much every Queensite loved him.

Columbo was always disheveled, and he hunched over when he walked. He had one glass eye which he used to peer at witnesses and suspects with great effect. He would come across as extremely absentminded and incredibly awkward. Although he didn't look like the swiftest guy on two feet, he was smarter than everyone! He was truly a red-hot mess, but I loved him. He taught me something that I want to make sure you remember.

**If you are going to be a truly effective communicator you have to remember this last play.**

First, let me reminisce about how I learned it. I'd watch Columbo interview a suspect that I knew had committed the crime. After the interview, I'd see Columbo say good bye to the suspect and start to walk away! I'd start shouting at the TV, "No, no Columbo! What are you doing? You have found the right person! Don't tell me that this is going to be the time you let a bad guy get away!"

Just when I'd thought all was lost, Columbo would stop and hold his head for a few seconds like his thoughts were really hurting him. Then he would turn around slowly, gesture to the suspect, and say those iconic words:

"Just one more question!"

With that question, Columbo would solve the case! Justice was done! He was brilliant!

*Didjaknow* you can be brilliant, too?

How can Columbo help us with our communications? How does he help us win against digital distraction where we have *checked-out* even before we have left the virtual room? Of course, I am going to tell you!

Years ago, I started to pay close attention to my conversations. I wanted to figure out what enabled me to change the tone and outcome of an awkward interaction or a difficult conversation. What was the key factor that allowed me to turn around a challenging situation or relationship? Most importantly, what helped me to establish trust in my various roles in schools, human resources, training, and consulting? What worked were all skills that Columbo used:

- Listening
- Exhibiting a genuine interest in the person
- Having a healthy sense of curiosity
- Taking time to find out more detailed information
- Asking one more thoughtful question

I found that my *last question* was not a request. And it wasn't about me. The question was meant to show that I acknowledged the person and their experience.

Like Detective Columbo, my "one more question" showed others that I was really listening and paying attention. This was the question that showed empathy, acknowledgement, appreciation, or understanding.

Sometimes asking that "one more question" revealed how I and others were connected in amazing ways, beyond anything that social media could accomplish.

In reality, the "one more thing" didn't have to be a question. It could be a comment, but it had to be something that conveyed that I had been listening closely and was acknowledging something I had learned from the other person. This is a communication skill that can be used anywhere. In this digital era of distraction, people recognize its value and appreciate it.

Here is one example. I was returning from Upstate New York and was driving on Route 287 South just north of the city. Suddenly, traffic came to a dead stop and I was now part of a horrible, massive traffic jam with thousands of people stuck at a standstill for twenty miles in both directions. I couldn't get to the exit ramp. The only thing I could do was turn off the car and wait. I was trapped in a sea of cars for hours!

At first, I made the best of my situation and made phone calls and checked emails. I did some writing. Then I cleaned and reorganized my handbag, tote bag, and the glove compartment. I even dusted my car's interior! Finally, I ran out of things to do and looked around for a new activity.

I got out of my car and stretched my legs. I greeted the guy who had just emerged from the next car, and we began to chat. When we had finished talking about the traffic situation, and it appeared the conversation was over, I asked one more question.

"So where were you headed before all of this happened?"

He responded "Nanuet, New York."

My ears perked up. "Really? What a coincidence. My husband works in that town. He's a teacher."

A moment later he tells me, "I work with your husband."

It gets even better! While we were chatting, another man walked up to us. He told us that he had been on his way to his company. His division was closing, and this was going to be his last day of work. I was familiar with his area of expertise so we chatted for a bit. I shared a few referrals. When we saw that the traffic was starting to move, I gave him my card as we parted ways.

Giving him my card was "one more thing."

I didn't realize how small our world can be until later. I was on a conference call with a colleague. When I told my friend about the traffic jam I had endured and the conversations I had with various people, he replied, "I know that you had a long day, so you better be sitting down. I know that guy from the company that's closing. I coached him and his team."

So there you are! Two random conversations in a sea of cars, and I uncovered multiple connections. But none of it would have been revealed if I hadn't asked *one more question.*

It only takes a moment to ask that final question, but you have to be listening along the way to know what to ask. I can tell you have been listening throughout this playbook. And now I can sense you're all emotional with appreciation that we have reached this amazing depth of communication.

*Fuhgetaboutit.*

# The Winning Plays

Using my *Learned-it-in-Queens Communications Playbook* has helped me to build trust and understanding. I'm *Winning Against Digital Distraction*. The plays will help you too.

1. Keep in Authentic
2. When Stuck, Try Something New
3. Hey, Take A Breath
4. Hold on to Your Inner Child
5. Admit it, Sometimes You Get It Wrong
6. Find *Your* Front Stoop!
7. Ya Gotta Eat!
8. Ask One More Question!

Remember, this is not an intellectual exercise. To actually receive positive lasting effects from this book, you have to practice these plays! Give them a try.

But if you think you have a *bettah* way, I got one question for you: ***Whatayatalkinabout?!***

**Goodbye for Now**

We are getting to the end, but I'm still here. Did you think I had left, and that I was done talking? Nope. I'm not a flat leaver (a person who leaves in a lurch without a goodbye). I haven't run out of things to say about people and the way they communicate, but I am running out of pages. So, I want to use my last bit of space to say thank you for reading this little book.

To help me say goodbye, I invite you to become an honorary Queensite. You already know the accent. Now, all you have to do is keep it real, and listen and connect with others on your stoop, which doesn't have to be an actual "stoop." Then just keep *bettahing* your best.

Was that enough? It doesn't feel quite right. It was too short. There wasn't enough feeling. It doesn't *feel* like a real Queens' goodbye.

Usually we start saying goodbye in the house and that takes an hour. Then everyone has to walk down to where you parked your car. Once there, someone has to start discussing the color of your car or the fact that you did a decent job parking and didn't hop the curb and damage the front of the house like the last person who visited. Then there has to be a big discussion about what roads you're going to take to get home. At some point, a driver who has stopped his car in the street and has been waiting patiently for a parking spot will roll down his window and lean out of his car and shout, "Are you leaving or what?" Then the night is over.

It finishes with a kiss, a hug, a wave, and a Queens' goodbye for now.

# Welcome to The Learned-it-in-Queens Communications Playbook's Workbook Section

# Prologue

When I started writing "The Learned It-In-Queens Communications Playbook – Winning Against Digital Distractions" I was on a mission to challenge readers to adopt simple and effective ways to make our digital our communications bettah! (better). One of my recommendations was to find ways to create "Front Stoop Moments"[*] where you could conduct civil *"in your space"* conversations versus *"in your face"* interactions. I was all geared up to present and coach about how to leverage the best out of ourselves in in-person real time conversations.

Then the COVID19 Pandemic arrived and it impacted every aspect of our lives. If I thought I learned a lot about communication challenges growing up in Queens, I know that I learned a massive amount about our communications and the importance of human connection in our home (aka bunker) during COVID19.

We had to figure out how to address every part of our life from work, health, shopping, and socializing. My husband started to work from home, teaching High School Calculus[**] classes working diligently with his faculty so they could provide their students with the best experience they could under the circumstances.

This Irishman who "never met a sentence he couldn't make longer" now demonstrated that he never met a sentence he could not make *louder*. Every day, he taught calculus and held faculty meetings in the room directly below me or outside my home office's window. I could hear every word and every equation no matter if I closed the door or window or not. My husband's verbal presence was testing my nerves and challenging my

*Stoop -is a Dutch word for the "front steps"*
***Joe, who remembers period very differently has been quoted as saying "I was dat bad."*

ability to follow my own communication guidance to "engage in calm, focused, conversations" that I was dispensing on podcasts, conferences and blog posts.

I would often be heard telling colleagues and friends "I am surprised the neighbors have not come to the house to request adult learning credits, because *everyone* within a 50 yard radius could hear him teach!" Yes, the neighbors not only learned calculus, they also learned how to run a math department.

Like many of you, attending Zoom meetings became a daily fixture. More times than I can count, I was chided to "unmute" or "turn your camera on." I also learned about what it meant to be "camera ready" and "what not to do" as I served as a grip, a lighting and sound technician, as well as hair, make-up, and wardrobe. By month three, I had developed an everlasting appreciation for trained professionals. By month four, I started to wonder if I qualified for any union memberships.

Eventually, I figured out how to retrieve people from break out rooms and not disappear into my virtual backgrounds. And I learned that new friendships and professional relationships could be forged and retained in a two-dimensional world.

**Note:** Let me not forget to mention that this period provided me with an even greater appreciation for how fortunate I am to have my home, husband, health, and a network of people who strive to be their best and bettah every day. Just saying.

The following pages are all *about you*. This section is designed to help you to make the most of your personal interactions whether they be in person or online. I would like you to learn how to learn how to be intentional in your communications and how to identify opportunities to share small unscripted moments of connection, and energy as you provide others with your gift of listening and focus.

Everything else falls into place when we have that in hand.

The updated version of this playbook includes practice and planning worksheets so you can apply what you learned in the playbook. I've included quotes, reference tools and, of course, I mention food.

How can I write about having engaging conversations and creating connections without some mention of food? *Fuhgetaboutit.*

*Julienne*

# A Queens Style Code of Conduct Contract

Hey! I am talking to you! Yes, you!
We are not going anywhere before we work through a few details. As I told you before, New York City is a city of lawyers. One of our favorite past times is documenting what we said and to whom.

So how could I let you move forward without obtaining your signature on our rules of engagement? FYI, by writing your name and dating it, you are taking advantage of a pretty nifty bit of brain science.[***]

Read out loud or mutter the following points to yourself and fill in the blanks.

I promise (Your Name Here) that I will:

1. Appreciate my efforts to commit to learning
2. Not let my inner critic dominate my internal dialogue.
3. Remember that I get to be "this way" so it may take a little bit of time to sort myself out.
4. Be honest with myself and write down the first thing that comes to mind when I read the action prompt,
5. Not "edit and censor"[****] my comments because I know that any thought or "ideah" that popped into my head landed there for a reason.
6. Be open to viewing myself and others with a fresh perspective.
7. Conduct do-overs[*****] because nothing can improve without practice.
8. Use my new habits and behaviors to make a difference! (Aka so you can stop bugging other people!)

9.  Have some fun

10. Create Front Stoop Moments******

I am aware that I have communication challenges that require my attention and *pinkie- swear******** to uphold to practice and adhere to this Code of Conduct

Name _______________________________________________

(Print your real name *not* an alias)

Signature /Date _______________________________________

***     *How Does Writing Affect Your Brain? - NeuroRelay*
****    *I made up this expression years ago*
*****    *an opportunity to try something again in order to improve a  performance or a score.*
******    *Front Stoop Moments  See Play # 6*
*******    *https://en.wikipedia.org/wiki/Pinky_swear*

# The Learned-it-in-Queens Communications Playbook's Workbook

You purchased this book because you recognize the importance of developing good digital and in-person communication skills and habits. This workbook section is designed to be a place where you can reflect on your current communication habits and plan how you are going to implement what you've learned in Plays #1 - 8.

## Play # 1 Keep It Authentic

How can you "show up" the best way you can?

Let's begin by thinking of three (3) situations where you feel comfortable and at ease when you are communicating with others.

*Example*: I am always comfortable speaking to my best friend Jesse, because she listens and doesn't interrupt when I am describing a situation.

Provide your examples in the space provided below.

Example #1.

Example #2.

Example #3.

What is it about these situations that allowed you to feel comfortable?

What method of communication were you using in those situations? (i.e., in-person, text, etc.?) Why?

Provide some details in the space provided below.

*Example*: They didn't look at their phones when we had an in person conversation.

What do these examples have in common?

*Example*: Everyone I wrote about is a good listener.

Provide your comments in the space provided below.

O.K. So far so good. Next! This is where it starts to get interesting.

Take a moment to think about three (3) communication situations that prompt you to experience some emotional discomfort and/or "hit your buttons!" (i.e. situations that cause you to feel uncomfortable, nervous, or even angry.)

Who are you communicating with and why?

What method of communication are you using (i.e., in-person, text, etc.?)

*Example:* My conversations with my colleague Theresa because she *informs* me what I should be feeling and dismisses my perspective. It's gotten so bad that I find myself texting Theresa so I don't have to listen to her make these annoying, breathing sounds when I tell her something.

Write your examples in the space provided below.

Example #1

Example #2



Example #3

Let's take a closer look at your examples and see if they have anything in common.

Provide your comments in the table provided below.

| Example # | The Situation | Communication Method | What I do? | How Do People React? (I.e. say, do or write?) |
|---|---|---|---|---|
| Example | I get very self conscious when I have to speak in front of a group of people in a meeting unexpectedly. | In person | I don't like to stand up.<br><br>I don't speak loud enough.<br><br>I fidget with my pen or papers. | They look down at the conference table.<br><br>Sometimes they interrupt with a question or a comment. |
| # 1 | | | | |
| # 2 | | | | |
| # 3 | | | | |

Think about what you just wrote in the section above. If you could do a Queen's (New York) style "do - over" what do you wish you could have done differently and why?

*Example:* I should prepare a few comments to have at the ready before I attend a meeting. I would practice saying them out loud. I am going to reach out to a coach for feedback about my presentation style so that I can be better prepared the next time.

Provide your comments in the space provided.

Great job being honest and getting your thoughts down on paper. This is a good start. Let's commute to Play #2.

## Play # 2 - Sometimes Our Communications Are Stuck and Just Aren't Moving Forward

What do you do when your conversations (live, digital or email interactions) are *not* moving forward in a *productive manner* and you feel "Super Stuck?"

In the section below describe your *super stuck* situations and what you are *doing* when your communications are not going as you wish.

**Important Note** - Don't write down that you take deep breaths and smile like an enlightened monk if this is not the truth! If your go-to reaction is to close your door and throw yourself on the floor and kick your legs in the air and yell – *own it*.

Provide your comments in the table provided on the next page.

| Example # | The Situation | Communication Method | What I do? | How Do People React? (I.e. say, do or write?) |
| --- | --- | --- | --- | --- |
| Example | People keep cutting me off during a group discussion | Virtual Meeting | I take my mobile out and I start scrolling through my social media. | They keep talking |
| #1 | | | | |
| #2 | | | | |
| #3 | | | | |

Who are you usually communicating with in these *"super stuck"* situations and why?

*Example:* My mother-in-law who works at my company, in fact, she owns the company. Awkward.

Provide your comments in the space provided.

- 

- 

- 

Is that all you're going to write? Are you sure that this is a complete list? I gave you plenty of room to share your thoughts, so feel free to challenge yourself and write more. If *you require inspiration or help,* consider reaching out to a spouse, partner, friend, colleague. I am *sure* that they will be *very willing to weigh* in and assist you as you work through this section. Just saying.

Finally, use the space below to write what you are *thinking* when things are not going your way when you are communicating.

Provide your comments in the space provided.

- 

- 

- 

Great job on taking the time to reflect and complete this section. Did you write anything that surprised you?

Do you see any patterns?


<u>Forward Action Prompt</u>

Complete the following section.

What I wrote in the previous sections contains valuable clues about my communication style and habits. I am going to practice doing the following moving forward:

- 

- 

- 

Completing this section was an important step! Great job. Onward.

**Important Note -** Reflection is an important activity and can yield many insights. It may also stir up emotions and memories. If writing these comments has unpacked some issues that you need to address that are more than poor communication habits, don't feel like you need to figure all of this out on your own. Seek the assistance of a licensed psychologist for support.

## Play # 3 Hey! Take a Breath

What do you do to take a pause so you can regroup and compose yourself when things get challenging? Do you run up and down the stairs? Sing? Watch silly videos on your mobile? My go-to regrouping activities are:

*Example:* I watch funny animal videos on UTube.

Write your responses In the space provided below.

- 
- 
- 

Circle the one that has been working the best. Why does it help you regroup?

Next, take a moment to revisit the activities that I listed in the "Play # 3 - "Hey Take a Breath" section on page 44.

Write the ones you're going to try and share the reason why. "The author told me to do this section " does qualify as a response.

*Example:* On page 43, I had suggested that when you found yourself feeling overwhelmed or perhaps over reacting, that you should consider converting your emotion into a donation* This way you'll do some good while you readjust your mental state.

Write your responses In the space provided below.

- 

- 

- 



Author's comment – What if everyone who read my book followed my guidance? Think about what the world would be like. Would there be less conflict? More dancing? More organized drawers and closets across the globe? Wouldn't that be a cool thing?

## Play #4 Assumptions and Your Inner Child

Here is the next challenge! Take a moment to own up to the assumptions you make about other people. Now take a few deep breaths and write down the assumptions that impact your ability to listen and communicate with others.

*Example:* I don't trust anyone who doesn't eat dessert. I find this type of self control very suspicious.

Share your thoughts in the space provided below.

- 
- 
- 

Complete the following sentence. My assumptions prevent me from:

*Example:* Being more curious and finding out what we do have in common.

Write your responses In the space provided below.

- 
- 
- 

We are not going to stay "stuck" in our assumptions, are we? No! We may not be able to eradicate them completely, but we can start by becoming more aware and taking small steps to change how they affect our interactions and even our self-perception.

*What am I going to change?*

The first assumption that I am going change is ______________________
because
If I do, I will be able to ____________________
I will accomplish this by becoming aware of
______________________________

and (doing or thinking) ____________________

Developing our awareness and making small concrete changes is so important. You are on the right path. Well done.

## Play #5 - Sometimes We Get It Wrong

Oh yes! I know! The fun just does not stop in this book! In the prior sections we described how our communications "get stuck" and what we can do to change those situations. We also acknowledged how our assumptions about others can impact our ability to listen and engage with them in a positive manner.

The funny thing about doing reflection exercises, memories about people and situations and people will begin to pop into our heads.

In the space provided below write down who you would like to and/or wish you could make amends with and why.

| Example # | The Situation | Communication Method | What I did? | How Do People React? (I.e. say, do or write?) | What I wish could do |
|---|---|---|---|---|---|
| Example | A workplace get together | An in-person conversation in a group setting | I teased someone about their abilities | The person stopped talking to me. | Take my words back and change how I talked about this person. |
| #1 | | | | | |
| #2 | | | | | |
| #3 | | | | | |

Remember that we agreed at the beginning of the workbook that we would be honest and own up to all of our messy bits. You did exactly that in this section. That took courage. Now take a moment to reflect on what you learned.

## #6 Front Stoop Moments

In Play # 6, I called for us to find opportunities to create *Front Stoop Moments*, where we could conduct live *side-by-side conversations* instead of *"in your face"* interactions.

Write your responses In the space provided below.

I wrote that our communication goal is to provide others with our *"full-on-focus"* when we listen. If we concentrated on the *"the power of small things to make a difference"* we would make great strides in improving our communications and relationships.

Think of a relationship that could use some improvement.
Write the person's name. ______________________________

Now *"find the good or the gift."*

Write down one or two positive things you can say about this person.

*Example:* Our relationship taught me that it is important to step into the other person's shoes when I communicate.

**Your comments:** Don't know what to write? Share any thoughts or insights that come to mind.

_______________________________________________________

_______________________________________________________

What are some efforts on your part that could make a difference?

*Example*: I could seek that person's input so I can gain a different perspective. I could learn why s/he feels this way.

**Your comments:**

_______________________________________________________

_______________________________________________________

## Play #7 - You Gotta Eat!

Now welcome to my favorite topic. It's all about the food. Food creates moments of connection and dialogue. Food tells stories. The act of cooking for someone or sharing a meal is a HUGE communication bridge builder.

## The Food and Communications Exercise

Describe a time when you learned an *important* lesson when someone shared a dish of food from their culture or family traditions.

*Example*: My Queens neighbors taught me about the joy of sharing with others when they brought homemade jams, cakes and garden vegetables to our house. I love cooking for others and seeing them smile.

Who shared their food or cooked for you?


What was the dish? What was in it?


What did you learn?


How does this lesson show up in your life?


Do other moments come to mind? What lessons do they hold?

### #8 Ask One More Question

A well timed and phrased question can change everything.

In the space provided, describe a time when you asked, *"one more question"* and it revealed a shared connection or you learned some interesting facts that changed your relationship for the good.

*Example:* I attended a food expo in New York City and struck up a conversation with a baker. A few minutes into the conversation we discovered that she went to school in the Caribbean with someone that I know. It proved to me that it is a very small world.


Write your example here.


Is there another opportunity for you to do this again?


When are you going to try this again?

## You Finished!

Congrats for finishing the work pages. Think of these pages as a living document because how you answered these questions will change as you address your communication challenges. So, think about your responses as a starting point that will remind you what you'd like to address and why. Check out the additional resources too! Now what?

Remember how I asked you earlier in the book how you want to "show up" in your communications? Now that you've completed all the workbook exercises, how are you going to show up?

# Resources

# The Winning Plays

Using my *Learned-it-in-Queens Communications Playbook* has helped me to build trust and understanding. I'm W*inning Against Digital Distraction.* The *Eight Plays* will help you too.

1. Keep in Authentic
2. When Stuck, Try Something New
3. Hey, Take A Breath
4. Hold on to Your Inner Child
5. Admit it, Sometimes You Get It Wrong
6. Find Your Front Stoop!
7. Ya Gotta Eat!
8. Ask One More Question!


Remember, this is not an intellectual exercise. To actually receive positive lasting effects from this book, you have to practice these plays! Give them a try. But if you think you have a *bettah* way, I got one question for you: *Whatayatalkinabout?!*

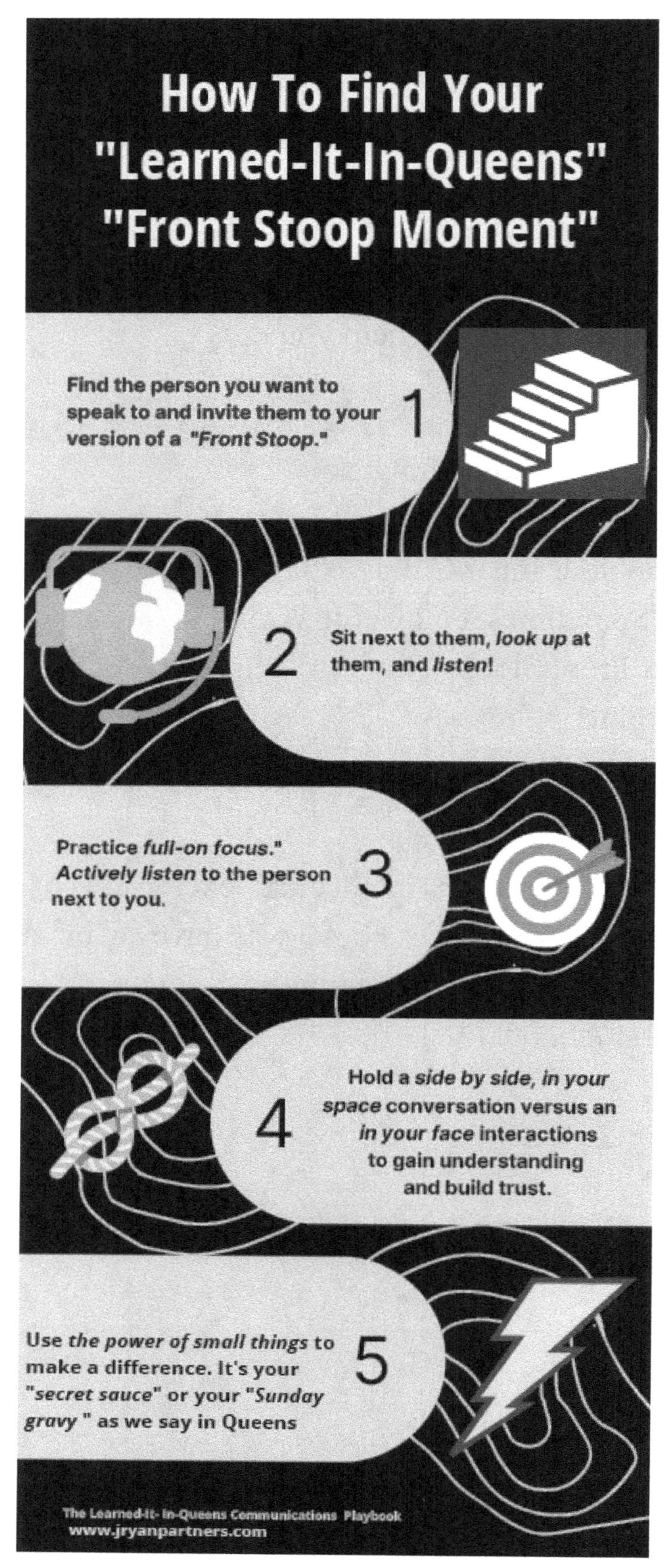
How To Find Your
"Learned-It-In-Queens"
"Front Stoop Moment"

Find the person you want to speak to and invite them to your version of a "Front Stoop."

1

2

Sit next to them, look up at them, and listen!

Practice full-on focus."
Actively listen to the person next to you.

3

4

Hold a side by side, in your space conversation versus an in your face interactions to gain understanding and build trust.

Use the power of small things to make a difference. It's your "secret sauce" or your "Sunday gravy " as we say in Queens

5

The Learned-It- In-Queens Communications Playbook
www.jryanpartners.com

# Queens, New York Celebrities - Communication Quotes

### Al Roker

"Always be yourself. At the end of the day, that's all you've really got; when you strip everything down, that's all you've got, so always be yourself."

### Awkwafina

"It's definitely a privilege to be able to do what you love to do; it's not something that everyone gets to do, so I feel really good about that."

### Bernadette Peters

"You've gotta be original, because if you're like someone else, what do they need you for?"

### Christopher Walken

"At its best, life is completely unpredictable."

### Cyndi Lauper

"It's a strange lesson to learn in life that your differences, the things that make you feel uncomfortable about yourself are what will help you to grow into who you are. Those are your gifts.

The more you practice and study, the better you are... so I still practice and study all the time."

### DJ Khaled

" Congratulations, you played yourself."

## Ella Fitzgerald

"What everyone wants more than anything else is to be loved"

## Ethel Merman

"When you are in deep conflict about something, sometimes the most trivial thing can tip the scales."

## 50 Cent

"You can't have a one-size-fits-all mind-set when it comes to effective leadership. You need to tailor a specific approach to every single person on your team in order to get the most out of them."

## Francine Drescher

"Your job is to get your audience to care about your obsessions."

## Groucho Marx

"Before I speak, I have something important to say."

## Howard Stern

"Nothing is casual. Everything requires work, research, and thought. Agonize. Take it seriously. Don't leave it up to someone else, and don't phone it in."

### Jerry Seinfeld

The advice I would give [the younger me]—or any young person—would be "Keep your head up in failure and your head down in success."

### John McEnroe

"You cannot be serious!"

**Jon Favreau**

"I think that anything that leads to creativity and good work is good."

**Jon Leguizamo**

"You think you've done it all, and then you realize, 'No, there's so much more to do."

**Louis Armstrong**

"We all do 'do, re, mi,' but you have got to find the other notes yourself."

**Lucy Liu**

"I think you just have to appreciate who you are and hopefully they can see what a superhero is about."

**Martin Scorsese**

"There's no such thing as simple. Simple is hard."

**Nicki Minaj**

"True confidence leaves no room for jealousy"

**Paul Newman**

"You only grow when you are alone."

**Ray Romano**

"You're only as good as your last joke, your last show, your last whatever. The confidence is there, but underneath, there is always insecurity."

**Rodney Dangerfield**

"I haven't spoken to my wife in years. I didn't want to interrupt her."

**Russell Simmons**

"Surround yourself with people who are smarter than you. ...

If you wake up deciding what you want to give versus what you're going to get, you become a more successful person."

**Spider-Man**
"With great power comes great responsibility."

**Tony Bennett**
"I still feel that I can get better somehow. And I search for it all of the "No matter where you're from or what you've done, you're never stuck in a particular circumstance, relationship, or cycle unless you say you are."

# Learning Library

## Podcasts

**Leadership Story Talks** – A podcast by Narativ – Co-Hosted by Julienne Ryan & Jerome Deroy, CEO Narativ

https://www.buzzsprout.com/1861177

https://www.youtube.com/@narativinc4338/videos

https://jryanpartners.com/podcasts/


## Books

Powered by Storytelling: Excavate, Craft, and Present Stories to Transform Business Communication – Murray Nossell, Phd

https://www.amazon.com/Powered-Storytelling-Excavate-Transform-Communication/dp/1260011909

Elements of Persuasion – Richard Maxwell & Robert Dickman

https://www.amazon.com/Elements-Persuasion-Storytelling-Better-Business/dp/0061179035/ref=sr_1-1

STFU: The Power of Keeping Your Mouth Shut in an Endlessly Noisy World - by Dan Lyons

https://www.amazon.com/STFU-Power-Keeping-Mouth-Endlessly

Innovating for Diversity: Lessons from Top Companies Achieving Business Success through Inclusivity by Bertina Ceccarelli and Susanne Tedrick

https://www.amazon.com/Innovating-Diversity-Companies-Achieving-Inclusivity/dp/

Reclaiming Conversation – The Power of Talk in a Digital Age – Sherry Turkle.
https://www.amazon.com/Reclaiming-Conversation-Power-Talk-Digital-ebook/dp/B00SI0B6PC

Emotional Intelligence: Why It Can Matter More Than IQ - by Daniel Goleman
https://www.amazon.com/Emotional-Intelligence-Matter-More-Than-IQ


## Collaborators

Jerome Deroy, CEO Narativ, Inc.
https://narativ.com

Naigu Bihalek, Founder- AccuMatch Behavior Intelligence
https://accumatchbi.com

Michael T. Holmes, CEO - Insight4U
https://www.linkedin.com/in/michaeltholmes

Maurelhena Walles, Founder - Equity by Design
https://www.equitydesigninc.com

# Now What?

You've done the work.

You've made it to the to the real end of the book.

But guess what?

It's really *"the beginning of the beginning"* of your new approach

to your communications.

It's a daily practice.

Keep showing up. Keep trying.

# About the Author

Photo of Julienne B. Ryan by Alex Berg

**Julienne B. Ryan** grew up in Queens having three communication choices: be funny, fight, or run really fast. Ironically, everything she wanted to dismiss, avoid, or forget about her formative years has become useful now. Like a one-woman sustainability project, she now encourages people to try appreciate the parts of themselves that make them unique. Besides being a writer, she is an organizational storyteller, a keynote speaker, a facilitator, soft-skills trainer, coach, and—*youBETTAhavenoticed*—humorist. Married for decades to a Dublin Irishman. Most of what she's learned about communicating, patience, and performing comes from living with him, a man who never met a sentence he couldn't make longer. She's been trying to get a word in edgewise for years, walking around looking like a 1960's Motown backup singer, holding up her hand so she could distract him. If she times it right, she can say a few words between his inhalations. But she has to be quick.

As her husband often heard her say during one of their lively discussions, "I've had me book learning."

She thanks the faculty at Manhattan College where she received her BA in Psychology & Urban Studies, and Teachers College at Columbia University where she earned her MA in Organizational and Development Leadership. She is a certified AccumatchBI Coach and certified Collective Brains Mentor and is trained Narativ Method Facilitator.

Learn more about Julienne Ryan and her keynotes, workshops, podcasts and coaching practice at: www.jryanpartners.com

Photo credit Julienne Ryan